MY JOURNEY INTO ARTIFICIAL INTELLIGENCE

ACTIVITY BOOK

DREAMLAND PUBLICATIONS
J-128, Kirti Nagar, New Delhi - 110 015, India
Tel.: +91-11-2510 6050, 2543 5657
E-mail : dreamland@dreamlandpublications.com
Shop online at www.dreamlandpublications.com
Follow us on www.instagram.com/dreamland.publications

Published in 2026 by
DREAMLAND PUBLICATIONS
J-128, Kirti Nagar, New Delhi - 110 015, India
Tel : +91-11-2510 6050, 2543 5657
E-mail : dreamland@dreamlandpublications.com
www.dreamlandpublications.com

Printed in India

PREFACE

Welcome to "My Journey into Artificial Intelligence"!

Artificial Intelligence (AI) is not just a futuristic concept—it's a present-day reality that is reshaping the world as we know it. It isn't just in science fiction anymore—it's all around us, making our world smarter and more exciting. From virtual assistants on our smartphones to autonomous vehicles navigating our roads, AI is woven into the fabric of modern society, revolutionizing how we live, work, and interact with the world around us.

This book is your ticket to exploring the amazing world of AI! It is designed to introduce readers to the wonders of AI in a fun and engaging way. In these pages, we'll dive into the basics of AI and discover some of the cool things it can do. From robots that help us at home to computers that can understand what we say, AI is changing the way we live and work.

Get ready for an adventure! We'll learn about AI in a fun and interactive way, with activities and experiments that will spark your imagination and curiosity.

So, are you ready to join me on this journey into Artificial Intelligence? Let's go!

CONTENT

CHAPTER 1: What is ARTIFICIAL INTELLIGENCE?

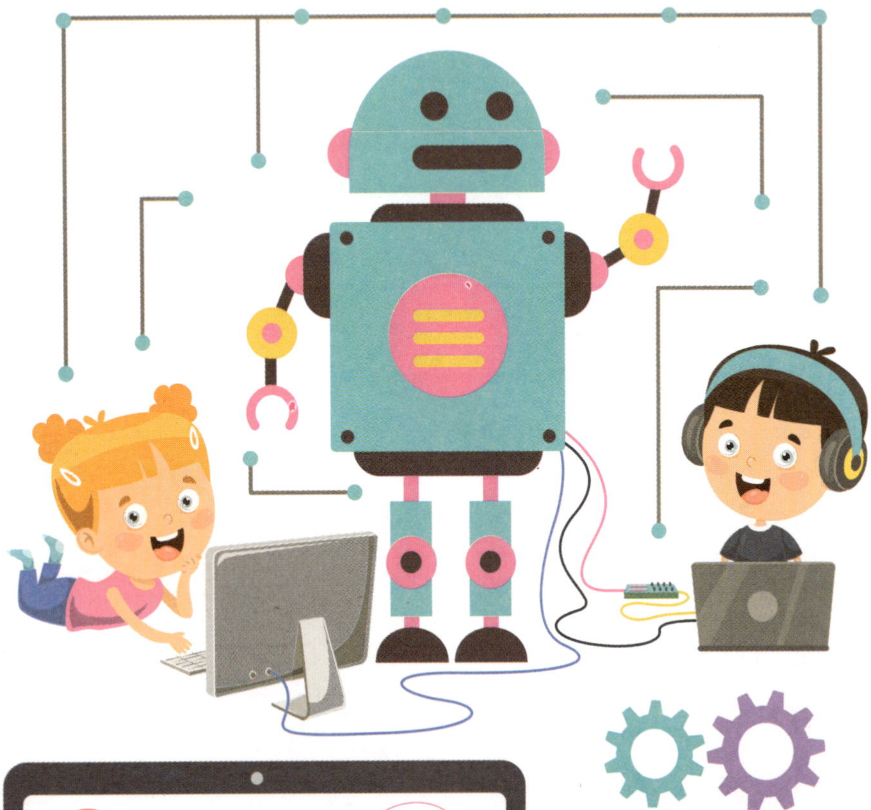

WHAT IS AI?

Imagine having a friend who can learn anything, remember everything, and think fast. This friend doesn't get tired and is always ready to help you. Now, imagine this friend is not a person but a computer or a robot. That's what we call Artificial Intelligence, or AI for short. AI allows machines to learn from experience, adjust to new inputs, and perform human-like tasks. With AI, computers can solve puzzles, recognise pictures, and even play games!

AI IN OUR LIVES

Have you ever played a game on a Tablet or used a Smartphone to ask a question? Or you've seen a car that can drive itself. These are all examples of AI at work! AI is like magic in the technology world, making devices more intelligent to help us in new and exciting ways. From assisting doctors in diagnosing diseases to letting you play games with a computer as your opponent, AI is everywhere!

HISTORY OF AI

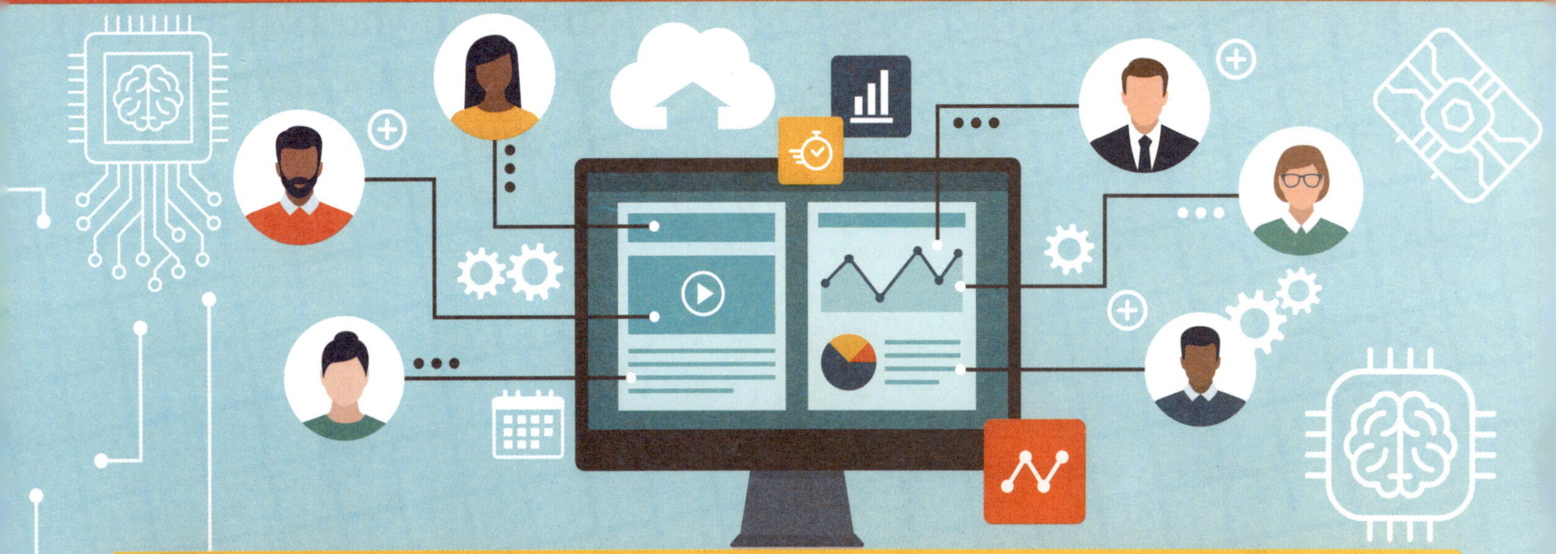

THE BEGINNING OF AI

Long ago, people could only dream about machines that could think. The story of AI began in the mid-20th century when scientists started to wonder if computers could be made to think like humans. They began creating machines that could solve problems and learn a little, like a baby learning to walk. This was the start of AI, and it was like the first step on a long, exciting journey.

AI GROWS UP

As years passed, AI grew smarter. In the 1990s and 2000s, computers began to beat humans at chess and answer questions on TV shows. Today, AI can do even more amazing things, like understanding what we say and creating art. It's like watching a child grow up to do things that surprise and amaze us. AI's journey is far from over, and the future is filled with endless possibilities.

DIFFERENT KINDS OF AI

Did you know there are different types of AI? Some are specialists, excelling at tasks like chess or math. Others are generalists, trying to learn a bit of everything. We call these Narrow AI and General AI. Narrow AI is like a super-smart bee making honey, while General AI is like a versatile superhero. Additionally, there's Artificial Superintelligence (ASI), surpassing human intelligence. ASI is a hypothetical future stage, sparking much debate. The field of Artificial Intelligence (AI) encompasses various approaches, but discussions often revolve around three main types. Other types include Reactive Machines, Limited Memory, Theory of Mind, and Self-Aware AI, each with unique capabilities and implications.

AI IN THE WORLD

You might wonder where all these AIs are. Well, Narrow AI is all around us! It's in your video games, helping cars drive themselves, and even in your home, controlling smart devices. General AI, the kind that's as smart as a human in every way, is still something scientists are working towards. It's like the final boss in a video game that we're all excited to meet one day.

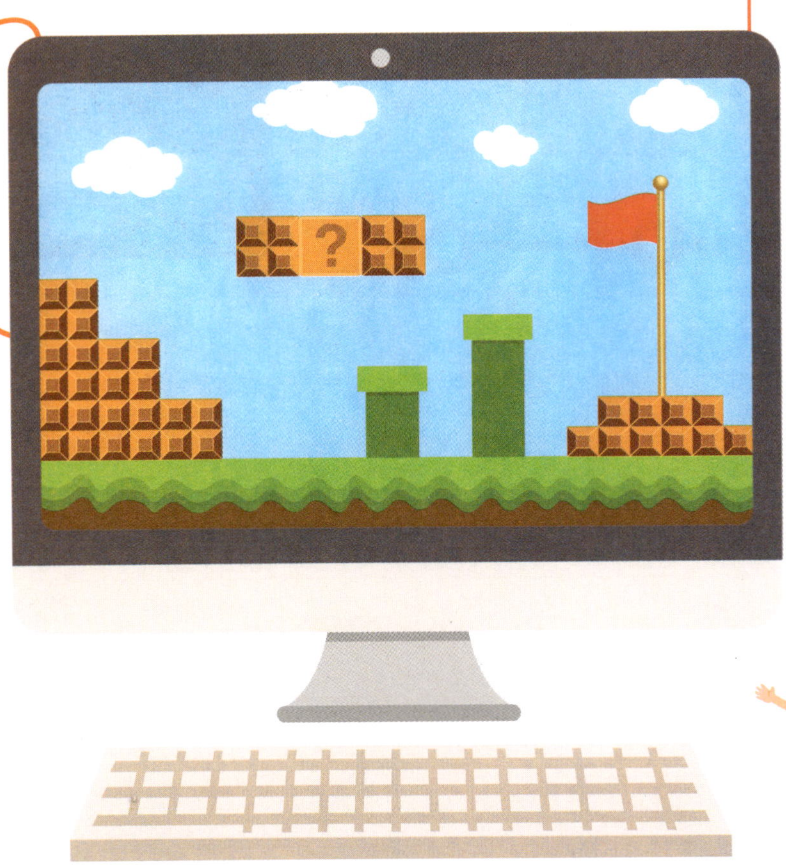

EXPLORING ARTIFICIAL INTELLIGENCE AROUND US

Now, let's go on an adventure! Find examples of AI around you. It could be anything from a voice assistant on your phone to a smart fridge that tells you when you're out of milk. Note down what you find and think about what kind of AI it might be. Is it a specialist, really good at one task, or is it trying to learn many things?

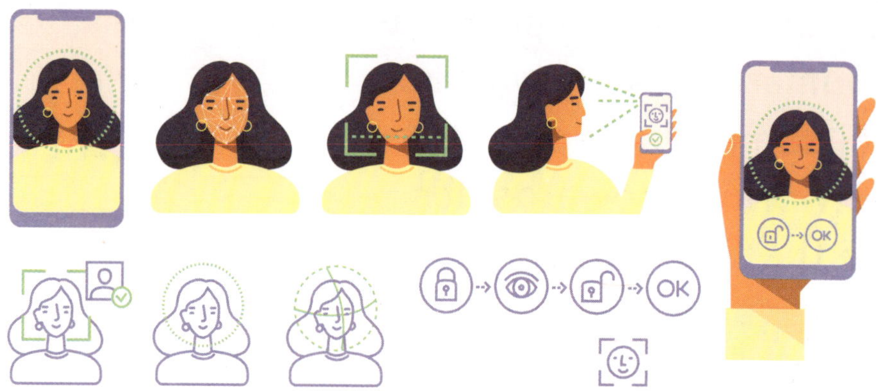

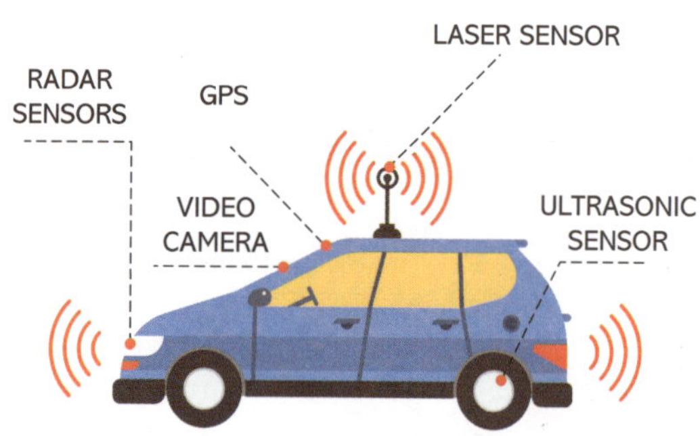

EXPLORING ARTIFICIAL INTELLIGENCE AROUND US

Explore different types of artificial intelligence (AI) and match each description with its corresponding name. AI comes in various forms, each with unique capabilities and applications. Test your understanding and see if you can correctly identify the types of AI based on their descriptions. Ready to embark on this AI adventure? Let's get started!

SPECIALISES IN PLAYING CHESS AND SOLVING MATH PROBLEMS.	THEORY OF MIND
AIMS TO LEARN BROADLY ACROSS VARIOUS DOMAINS.	REACTIVE MACHINES
SURPASSES HUMAN INTELLIGENCE AND IS A HYPOTHETICAL FUTURE STAGE.	SELF-AWARE AI
RESPONDS TO STIMULI IN REAL-TIME WITHOUT MEMORY OR LEARNING.	NARROW AI
CAN REMEMBER PAST EXPERIENCES AND USE THEM TO MAKE DECISIONS.	ARTIFICIAL SUPERINTELLIGENCE (ASI)
UNDERSTANDS THE BELIEFS, INTENTIONS, AND EMOTIONS OF OTHERS.	GENERAL AI
DEMONSTRATES SELF-AWARENESS AND CONSCIOUSNESS.	LIMITED MEMORY

CHAPTER 2: How DOES AI WORK?

WHAT IS DATA

Imagine if you could remember every single thing you ever saw, heard, or felt. Everything from the colour of the sky to the sound of leaves rustling in the wind would be information you could use. For AI, this kind of information is called data. Data is like food for AI; it helps AI learn and grow wiser. Just like you learn from reading books or listening to your teacher, AI learns from data. Data comes in all shapes and sizes: numbers, words, pictures, and even sounds. For example, when you take a photo with a smartphone, that photo becomes data that an AI can analyse to recognise faces or objects.

HOW AI USES DATA

You might wonder, "How does AI use all this data?" Well, let's think of it as a puzzle. When you first start a puzzle, it's a bunch of mixed-up pieces. But the picture comes together as you look at each piece and figure out where it goes. AI uses data as puzzle pieces to learn and make decisions.

For AI to recognise a cat in a photo, it must see many pictures of cats. Each image is a piece of data that helps the AI understand what a cat looks like. The more data it has, the better it gets at recognising cats, just like how you get better at puzzles the more you do them.

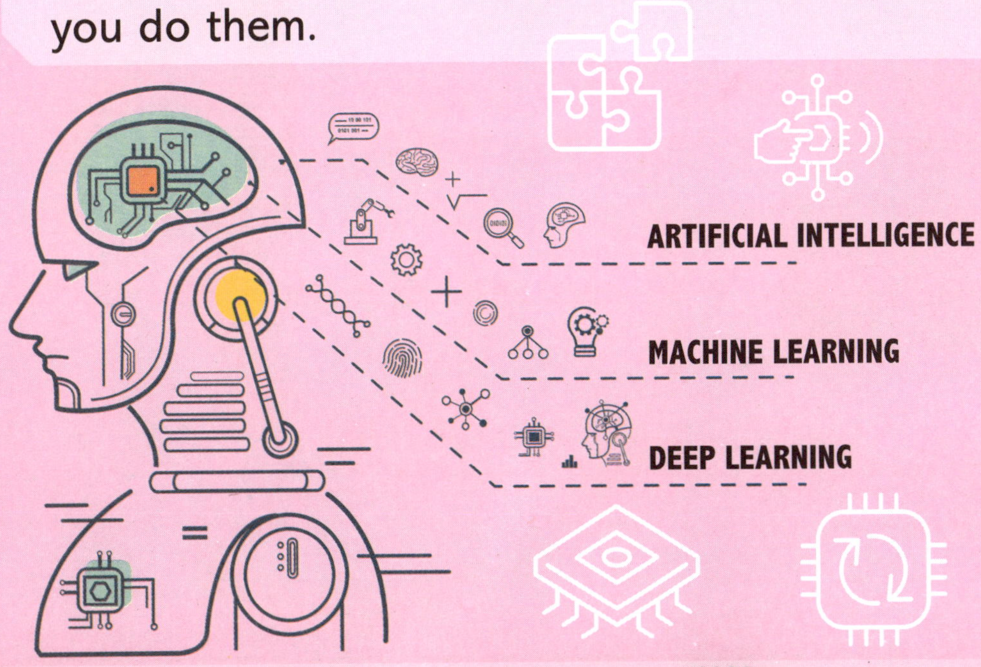

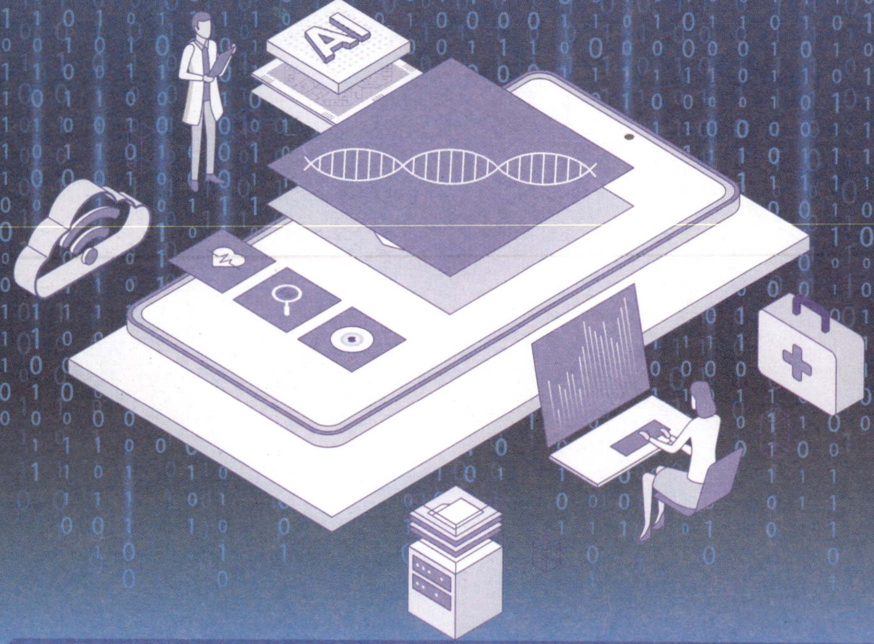

WHAT IS AN ALGORITHM?

An algorithm is like a recipe for AI. Just like how a recipe tells you step-by-step how to make a cake, an algorithm tells AI how to solve problems. For example, there's an algorithm for adding numbers, an algorithm for playing a game, and even an algorithm for suggesting which video you should watch next on the internet. Algorithms are the secret behind why AI can do so many amazing things. Scientists and engineers write these algorithms to help AI learn from data and make decisions.

MACHINE LEARNING

Machine Learning is when AI learns to do things independently without being directly programmed for every task. Imagine teaching a robot to clean your room. Instead of telling it every single step, like "pick up the socks, then fold the clothes," you let it watch you clean a few times. After watching, the robot learns the best way to clean up independently.

This is what machine learning does. It allows AI to learn from examples and improve over time. The more it practices, the better it gets, just like you with your homework or sports.

WHAT ARE NEURAL NETWORKS?

The human brain inspires neural networks. Just like your brain has many cells called neurons that work together to help you think, learn, and remember, neural networks in AI have "artificial neurons" that help computers learn and make decisions. These networks can learn from data, recognise patterns, and make predictions. For example, a neural network might learn to predict the weather by looking at patterns in temperature, wind, and clouds over time.

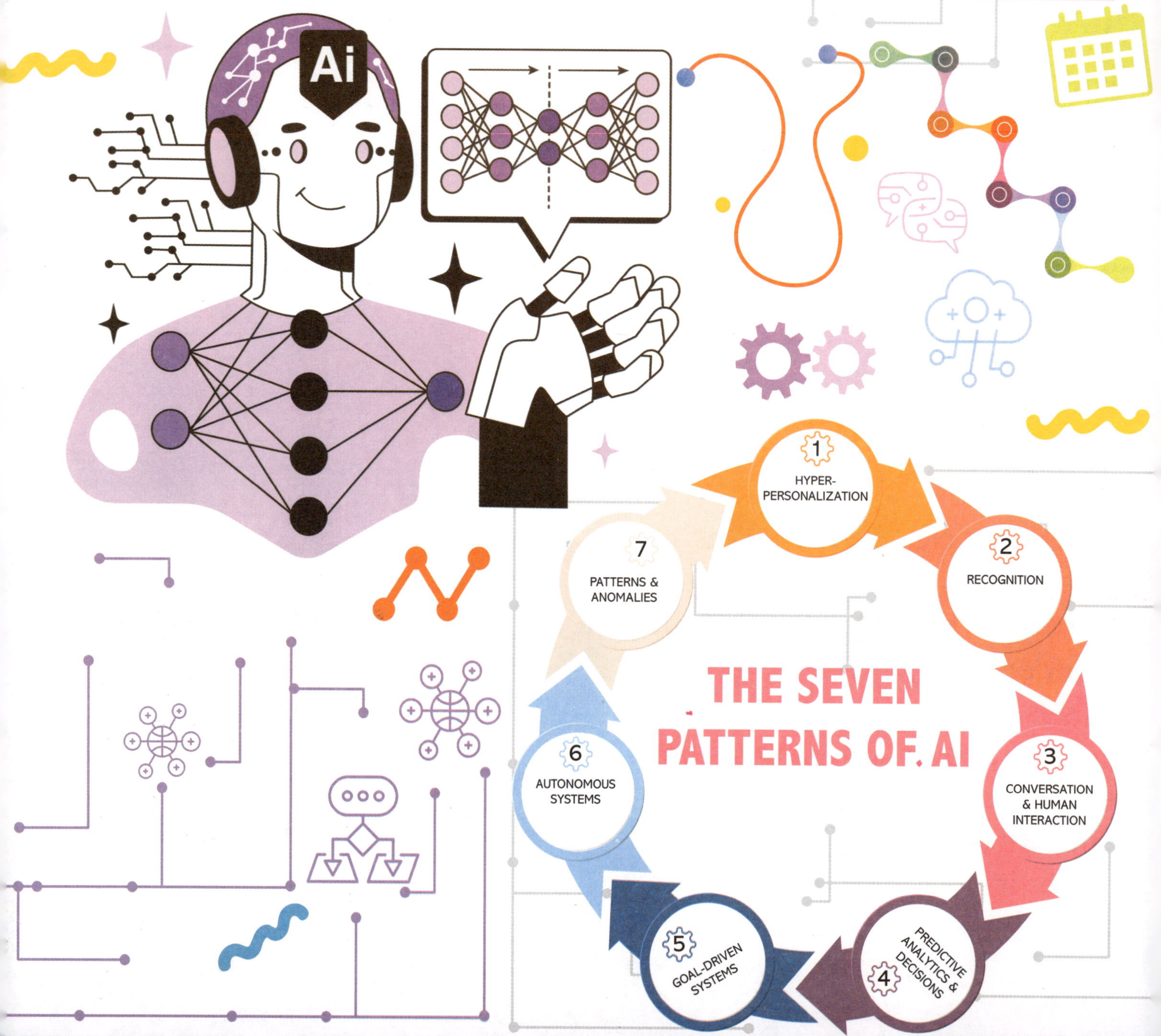

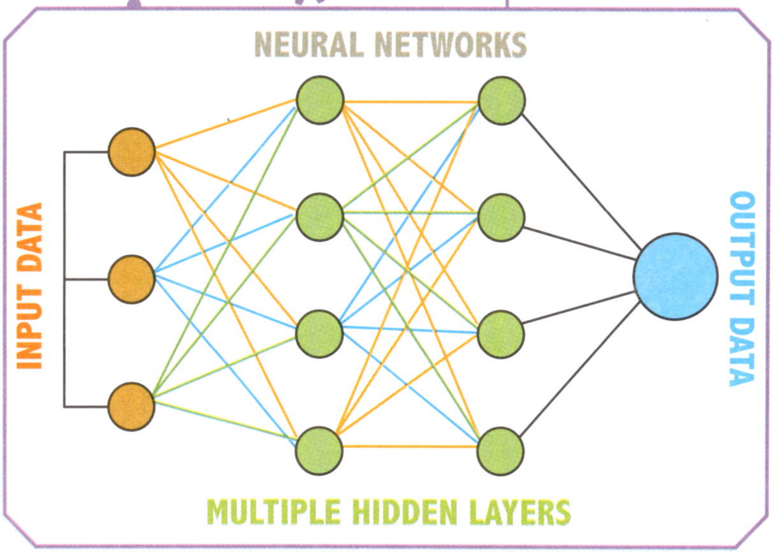

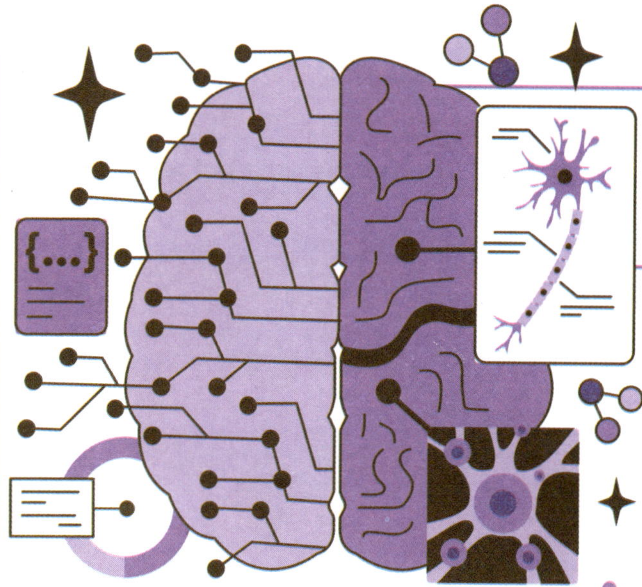

The featured image represents that how Neural Networks work.

Input layer: In this layer, we insert data.

Multiple hidden layer: Invisible layer which processes all the input data.

Output layer: Gives output of data that was inserted.

HOW NEURAL NETWORKS LEARN

Learning for a neural network is like learning to catch a ball. At first, you might miss a lot, but as you practice, your brain gets better at knowing where to put your hands. Neural networks learn similarly. They try to solve a problem, see how close they get, and adjust until they get it right. For AI, this process involves a lot of trial and error with data. By repeatedly practising with data, neural networks learn to recognise faces, understand spoken words, and much more. It's like a super-smart practice session that helps AI improve.

SHADOW GAME

Now it's your turn to think like AI! In this activity, you'll play a game where you have to find the right shadow for the robots.

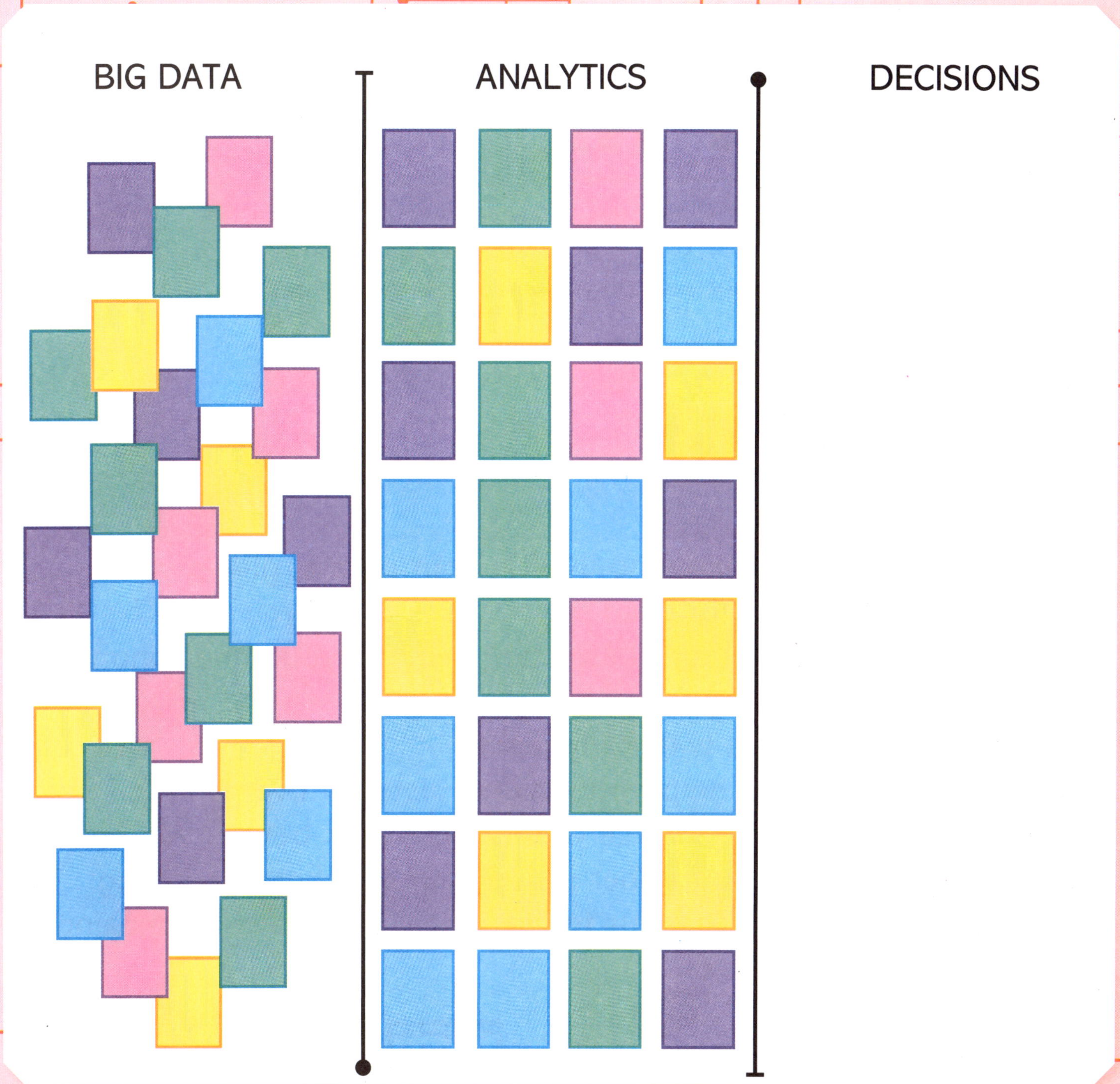

SHAPE SEQUENCER

This page is set up like a game board with different shapes and colours. Your challenge is to predict the next shape in a sequence based on the patterns you see. As you make your guesses, your "trainer" will tell you if you're right or wrong, helping you "learn" the pattern. This is a fun way to see how machine learning works by trying it out yourself!

CHAPTER 3: AI in EVERYDAY LIFE

SMARTPHONES AND AI

Imagine talking to a friend who lives in your phone, giving you answers, playing music, or even telling jokes when you ask. This friend isn't a person but an AI assistant living in your smartphone. AI allows your phone to understand your voice, respond to your questions, and help you with daily tasks.

AI in smartphones also helps with taking pictures. Ever wonder how your phone knows how to make your photos look better? AI works like a professional photographer inside your cellphone, deciding how to adjust the light or focus to make your photos look amazing.

MORE THAN JUST TALKING

But AI does even more on your phone. It learns what you like, suggests new games you might enjoy, or reminds you about your friend's birthday. AI is like a smart helper, always there to make your phone smarter and your life easier.

AI IN VIDEO GAMES

Have you ever played a video game where the characters seem to think independently? Maybe they chase you, hide, or even try to outsmart you. That's AI at work! Game developers use AI to create challenging, intelligent opponents and dynamic, ever-changing worlds.

AI also helps make games more fun by adjusting the difficulty. If you're doing really well, the game might get harder to keep you challenged. If you're struggling, it might get easier. This way, the game is always just right for you.

AI IN MOVIES AND MUSIC

AI isn't just in games; it's also in movies and music. Filmmakers use AI to create incredible special effects, like realistic-looking creatures or epic battle scenes. In music, AI helps composers develop new songs or even create entirely new sounds.

AI IN HEALTHCARE

AI is like a superhero for doctors and nurses. It can look at X-rays and scans to help find illnesses like a super-smart detective finding clues. AI also helps researchers discover new medicines faster, saving more lives.

AI AND THE ENVIRONMENT

AI helps our planet too. It can predict weather disasters, assisting people to stay safe. AI also figures out better ways to use energy, making everything from cars to factories cleaner and greener. It's like an eco-friendly helper, always looking for ways to protect our Earth.

AI IN EVERYDAY LIFE

Now it's your turn to be an AI detective! Your mission is to find AI in your daily life. This could be anything from a smart thermostat that adjusts the temperature to a website that recommends videos. Use the images as clues and complete the crossword puzzle.

AI DETECTIVE NOTEBOOK

Write down the names of the AI you find around you. How does it help people? How does it make things easier or more fun? Discuss your findings with friends or family, and see if they've noticed the same AIs in their lives.

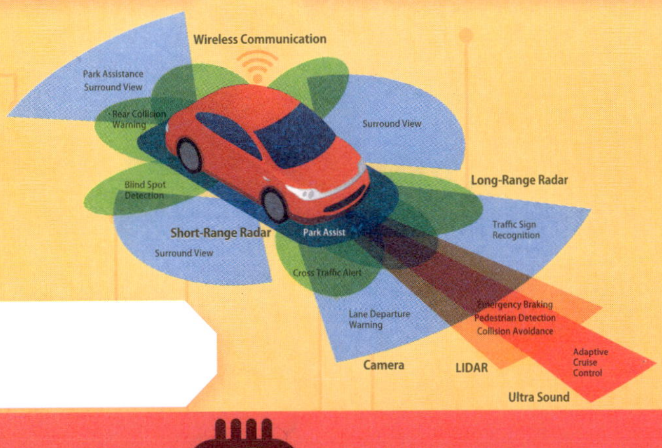

CHAPTER 4: Creative AI AND ART

AI, THE ARTIST

Did you know AI can create art? It's true! Artists and computer scientists have taught AI to paint pictures, design sculptures, and create animations. These AIs analyse thousands of artworks to learn different styles and techniques. Then, using what they've learned, they can create new pieces of art that have never been seen before. Some AIs can collaborate with human artists, combining people's creativity with the vast knowledge and speed of computers. This partnership can lead to fantastic new kinds of art that neither humans nor AI could create alone.

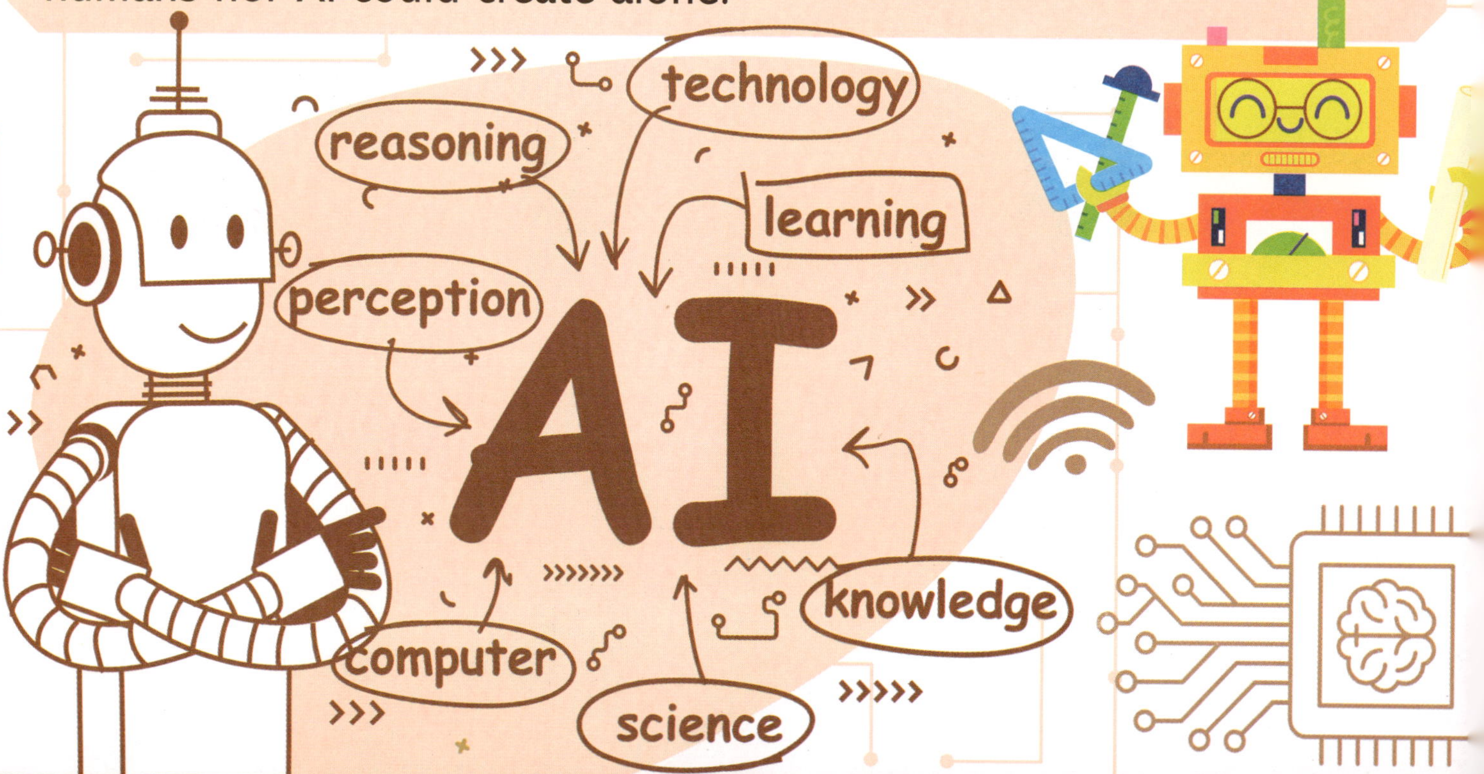

HOW AI CREATES ART

You might wonder how a computer can be an artist. Well, it starts with data. Like in other areas of AI, art-making AIs learn from many examples. Artists feed the AI images of paintings, sculptures, and other artworks. The AI studies these examples to understand patterns, colours, and shapes.

Then, the AI uses algorithms to generate its own art. It can mix and match styles from different artists or come up with entirely new ideas. Sometimes, the results are surprising, even to the AI's creators!

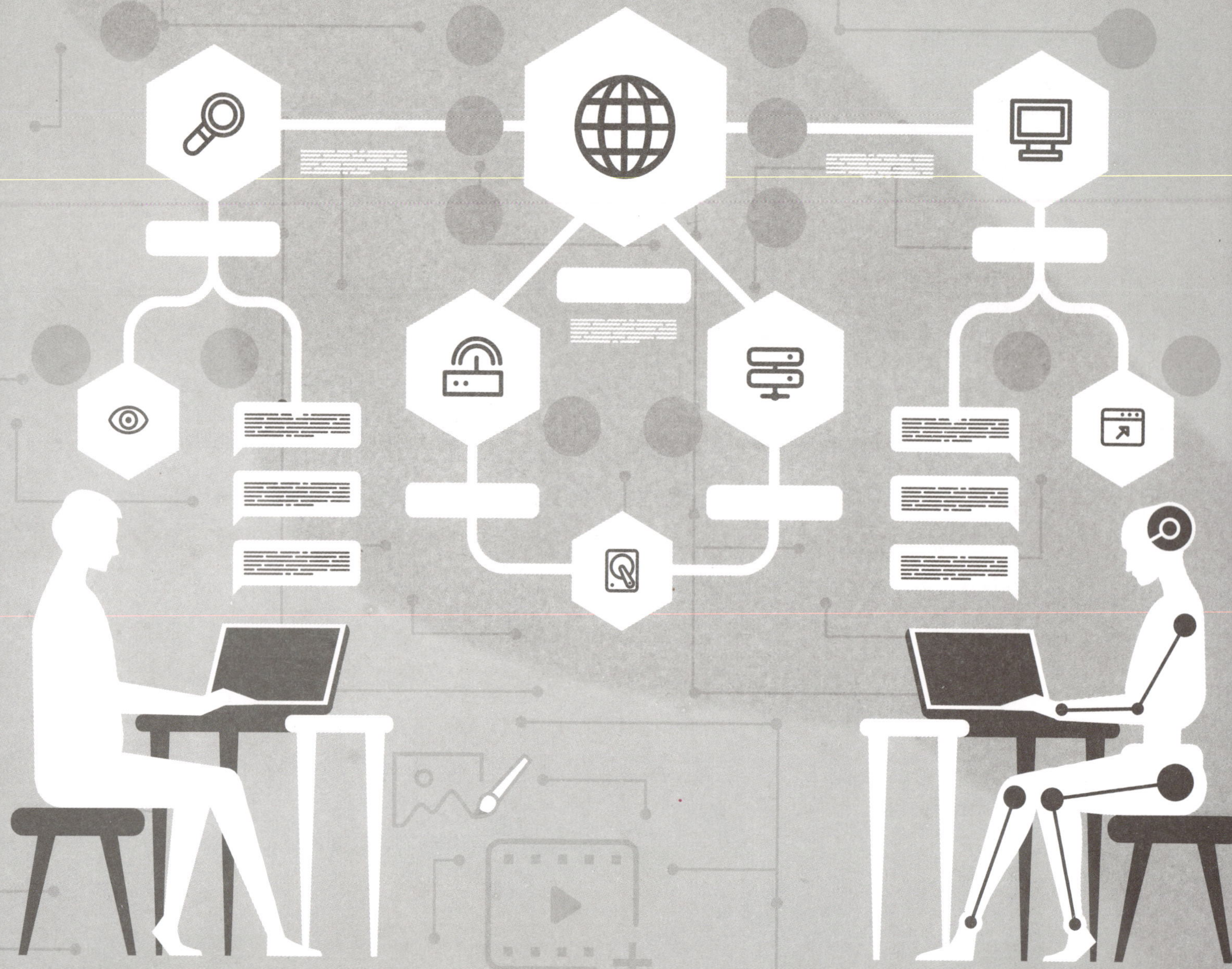

AI, THE STORYTELLER

AI is not just making waves in the world of visual arts but also in writing. Imagine a machine that can write stories, poems, or even movie scripts. AI writers can generate new tales based on guidelines given by human authors, like setting, characters, and plot points. These AI systems learn from reading a vast amount of text—from classic novels to modern blogs. They understand language patterns, storytelling structures, and even humour. With this knowledge, they can craft stories that entertain, intrigue, and inspire.

THE MAGIC OF AI WRITING

The process of AI writing is like mixing ingredients to bake a cake. First, the AI takes in all the "ingredients" (words, phrases, story arcs). Then, using algorithms, it "bakes" these ingredients into something new and exciting. While AI-written texts might not always have the emotional depth of those written by humans, they can spark ideas and offer new perspectives. Writers often use AI to overcome writer's block or generate creative story prompts.

AI, THE INVENTOR

AI doesn't just create art and stories; it also invents new things. From designing shoes and clothes to creating new recipes, AI's ability to analyse data and recognise patterns makes it a powerful tool for innovation. Engineers and designers use AI to explore countless design possibilities in seconds, something that would take humans much longer. AI can simulate how a new product would work, helping creators refine their ideas before making an actual prototype.

AI'S ROLE IN INVENTION

Imagine trying to invent a new kind of sneaker. AI can help by analysing thousands of existing shoe designs, materials, and customer reviews to suggest improvements or new concepts. It can also test the new design's durability or comfort without building it first. This way, AI is a creative assistant, offering insights and speeding up the invention process. It enables inventors to push boundaries and devise solutions to problems we might have yet to think of.

COLLABORATIVE AI ART ADVENTURE

Welcome to the Collaborative AI Art Adventure! Get ready to unleash your creativity by collaborating with AI to create unique artwork.

CHOOSE AN IDEA: Think of a picture idea, like a futuristic city or a magical creature.

ACCESS AN AI ART TOOL: With adult supervision, explore these free AI art tools available online such as DeepArt.io, Artbreeder, or ChatGPT.

INPUT YOUR IDEA: Describe your concept or upload reference images to the AI too.

LET THE AI CREATE: Watch as the AI generates artwork based on your idea.

TAKE A PICTURE: After the AI has created the artwork, take a picture of it and paste it in the space provided.

MATHEMATICAL ARTISTRY

Help the robot reach the control panel by choosing the numbers strategically that end with a sum of 24.

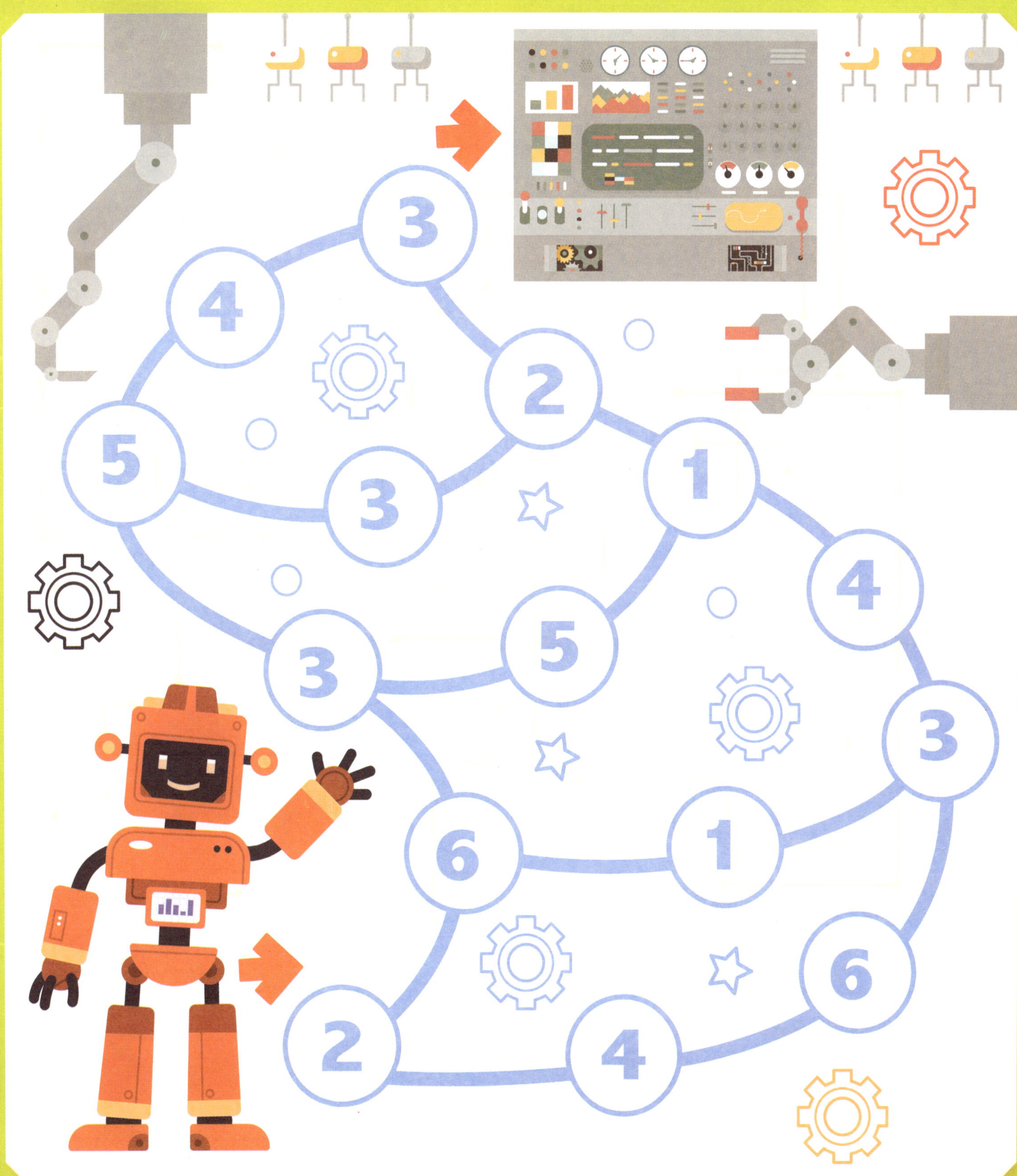

CHAPTER 5: The Future OF AI

WHAT'S NEXT FOR AI?

Imagine a world where robots and AI are part of everyday life, helping in ways we can only dream of today. Scientists are working on AI that can solve some of the world's biggest challenges, like curing diseases, protecting the environment, and exploring outer space. The future of AI is not just about making machines smarter; it's about using these technologies to make our world a better place. AI might change how we attend school, making learning more personalised to each student's needs. Imagine having an AI tutor who knows exactly what you find easy or hard and helps you learn at your own pace.

AI AND EXPLORATION

The future of AI includes robots exploring places where humans can't quickly go, like the deepest parts of the ocean, the surfaces of other planets, and even inside volcanoes. These AI explorers can help us understand more about our world and beyond, discovering new things about nature, science, and the universe.

AI AT WORK

As AI becomes a more significant part of our world, it will change how we work. Robots might do some jobs, like driving cars or managing factories. But humans will still be included. Instead, new kinds of jobs will be created, jobs that we might not have imagined yet.

People will work alongside AI, using it as a tool to do their jobs better and more efficiently. For example, doctors will use AI to help diagnose diseases more accurately, and architects will use AI to design safer and more innovative buildings.

LEARNING FOR THE FUTURE

With the changing job landscape, learning skills like problem-solving, creativity, and working with technology will be more important than ever. The future will need people who can think of new ways to use AI, improve it, and ensure it's used responsibly. This means there will be exciting opportunities for those curious about how things work and how to improve them.

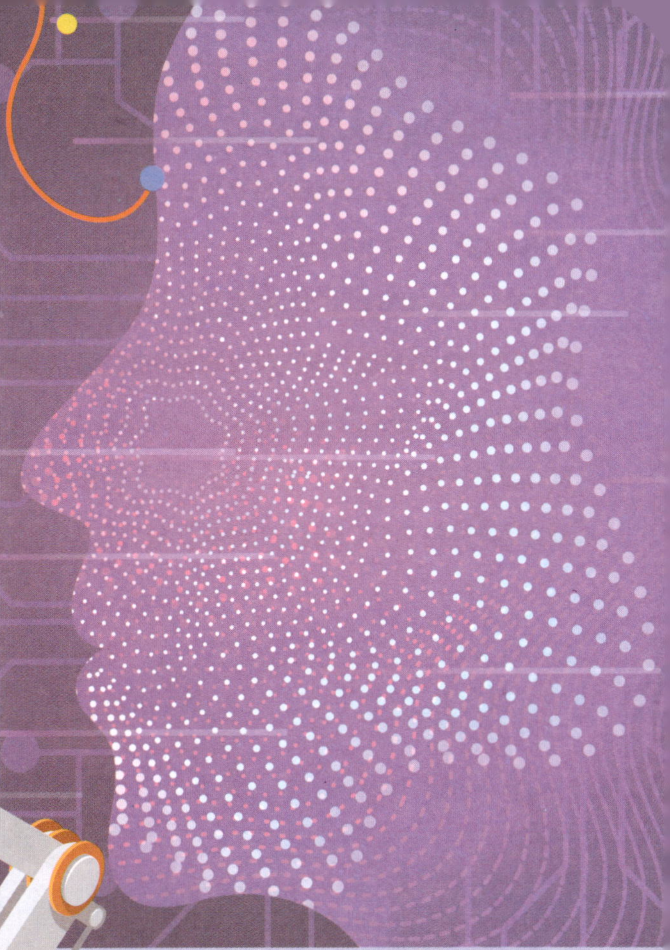

MAKING SURE AI IS GOOD FOR EVERYONE

As AI becomes more powerful, it's essential to ensure it's used in good ways for everyone. This means creating fair AI that doesn't discriminate and respects people's privacy. Scientists and engineers are working on rules to guide how AI is developed and used, ensuring it benefits society and does not cause harm.

YOUR ROLE IN AI'S FUTURE

How do you fit into the future of AI? Well, the future of AI is not just up to scientists and engineers; it's up to all of us. By learning about AI, thinking about how it should be used, and even getting involved in creating it, you can help shape a future where AI improves the world. Your ideas, creativity, and values will be important in ensuring AI is used in the best ways possible.

AI PRODUCTS SHAPING TOMORROW

Artificial intelligence (AI) has transitioned from a futuristic notion to a present-day reality, significantly altering our lives. With continuous advancements, AI is reshaping our daily routines, optimizing operations, and sparking innovation across various sectors. Below are some innovative AI products revolutionizing our lifestyles, professional environments, and interactions with the world:

AMAZON ALEXA: A voice-activated virtual assistant developed by Amazon.

TESLA AUTOPILOT: An advanced driver assistance system developed by Tesla, Inc.

GOOGLE ASSISTANT: A virtual assistant developed by Google that utilizes voice recognition and natural language processing to perform tasks and answer user queries.

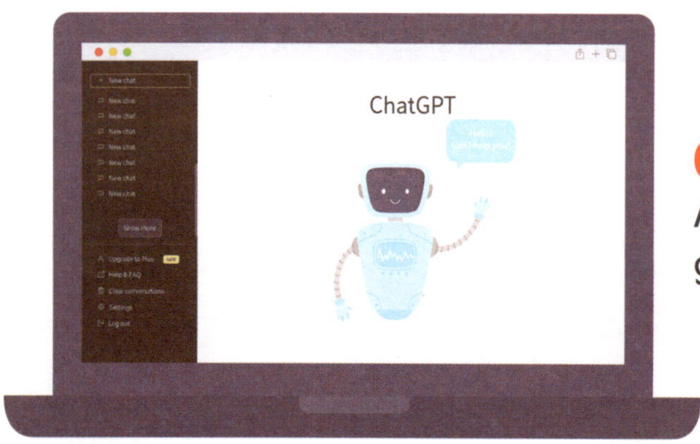

OPENAI'S GPT: A powerful AI language model capable of generating human-like text.

WAYMO SELF-DRIVING CARS: A pioneer in autonomous vehicle technology.

IBM WATSON HEALTH: An AI-driven platform designed to enhance healthcare by analyzing vast amounts of medical data.

RING VIDEO DOORBELL: A smart home security product developed by Ring, a subsidiary of Amazon.

THINKSTER MATH: An AI-powered online math tutoring platform.

BOSTON DYNAMICS' SPOT: An AI-powered quadruped robot developed by Boston Dynamics.

MINT: A personal finance app that utilizes AI to analyze users' spending habits and provide insights into their financial health.

LIVEPERSON: A customer service chatbot platform that uses AI to streamline customer interactions.

These pioneering solutions span various fields such as healthcare, education, retail, customer service, and beyond, exemplifying the boundless capabilities of AI.

ONE SHORT REVISION

1. What does 'AI' stand for?

(a) Artificial Intelligence (b) Artificial Inbuilt

2. What is AI?

(a) It is the ability for a computer to think and learn.

(b) It is a method to reach any academic or personal goal by following a few simple steps.

3. What tasks can computers perform with AI?

(a) Computers can perform tasks that are typically done by people.

(b) Computers can perform measurable outcomes.

4. Which search engine do people use every day?

(a) Google (b) Zoom

5. Why do doctors use artificial intelligence?

(a) To diagnose patients based on medical scans, like X-rays.

(b) To play with AI.

AI WORD HUNT

Find the hidden words related to artificial intelligence (AI) in the grid below. Words can be placed horizontally, vertically, or diagonally.

A	S	S	I	S	V	I	T	U	L	O	M	A	T	I
I	O	N	L	A	U	G	M	E	N	T	E	D	E	A
N	E	U	R	A	L	R	N	I	N	G	I	N	T	E
T	L	L	I	G	E	G	N	C	E	M	A	C	H	I
E	N	E	A	U	C	G	O	S	C	I	E	N	C	E
L	M	E	N	T	H	E	D	R	H	A	T	D	B	O
L	T	H	I	D	A	D	E	N	I	N	A	T	E	G
G	R	A	T	I	T	O	N	A	U	T	G	M	E	N
E	T	D	C	O	B	I	N	O	A	M	H	E	T	R
N	I	C	B	I	O	M	E	T	R	I	C	M	E	N
C	E	O	N	E	T	W	O	R	K	S	C	I	W	O
E	R	K	D	R	G	C	A	E	U	T	A	O	B	R
I	T	H	A	U	T	O	M	A	T	I	O	N	M	T
O	I	N	T	E	G	R	A	T	I	O	N	E	G	R
A	O	U	R	A	L	C	I	M	B	I	T	H	A	M

ROBOT | ALGORITHM | CHATBOT | AUTOMATION

BIOMETRIC | AUGMENTED | INTELLIGENCE | INTEGRATION

DATA | NEURAL | NETWORK | SCIENCE

BRAIN VS. BOTS

Match each task to the correct image of either the human brain or the robot, depending on whether you think humans or AI agents are better suited for the task. Draw a line connecting each task to the corresponding image.

Task	**Humans or AI Agents**
1. Processing large amounts of information	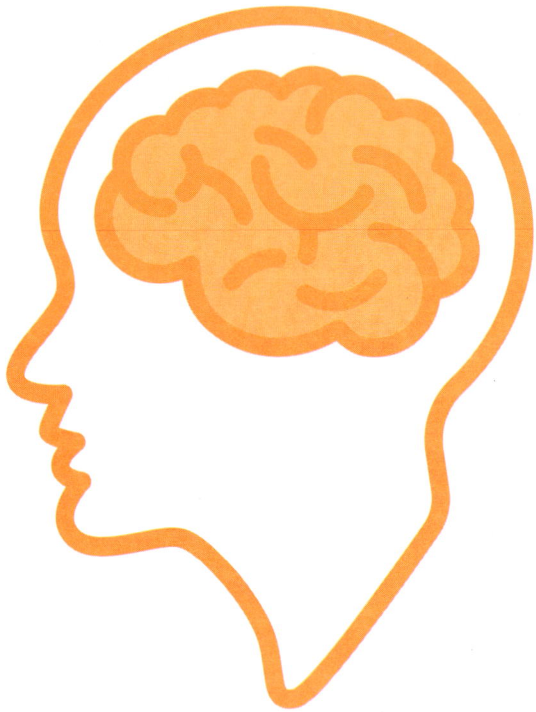
2. Providing support for emotional issues	
3. Showing Sympathy	
4. Monitoring stock control	
5. Managing and optimizing social media accounts	
6. Recognising and interpreting facial expression	

DESIGN YOUR AI ROBOT

Use your creativity to design your own AI robot. Describe the robot's features, functions, and how it will help you.

ANSWERS

ANSWERS WILL VARY

PAGE 10

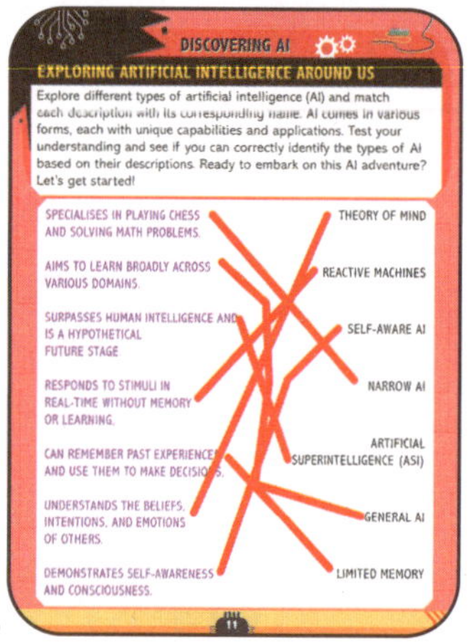

PAGE 11

PAGE 18

PAGE 19

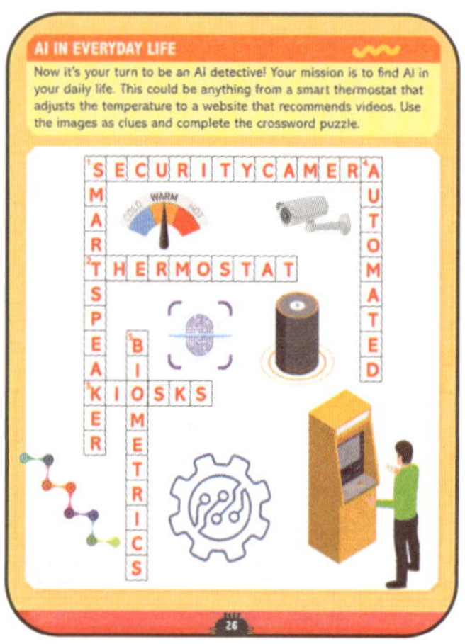

PAGE 26

PAGE 27

ANSWERS WILL VARY

PAGE 34

PAGE 35

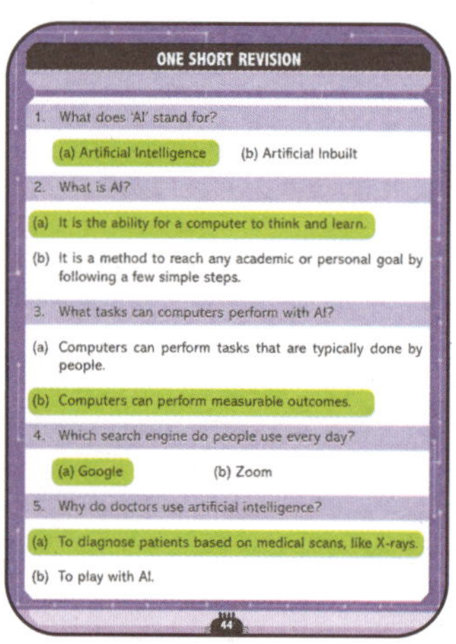

PAGE 44

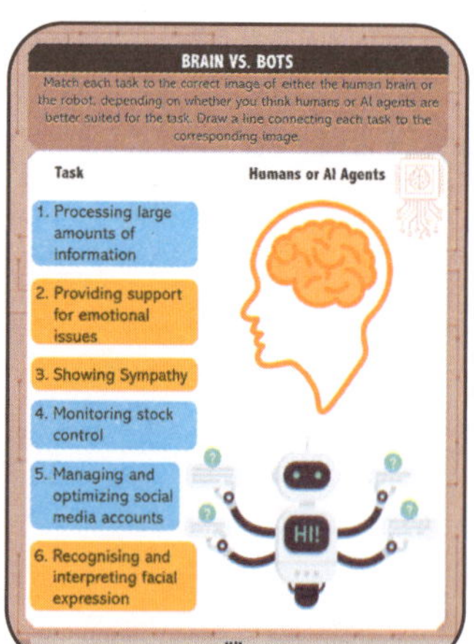

PAGE 46

ANSWERS WILL VARY

PAGE 47